In the Ghost-House Acquainted

((

Kevin Goodan

ALICE JAMES BOOKS

FARMINGTON, MAINE

10 9 8 7 6 5 4 3 2 1

Alice James Books are published by Alice James Poetry Cooperative, Inc.,
an affiliate of the University of Maine at Farmington.

Alice James Books
238 Main Street
Farmington, ME 04938

www.alicejamesbooks.org

Library of Congress Cataloging-in-Publication Data
Goodan, Kevin, 1969-
In the ghost-house acquainted / Kevin Goodan.
p. cm.
ISBN 1-882295-47-1
1. Pastoral poetry, American. 2. Country life--Poetry.
3. Farm life--Poetry. I. Title.
PS3607.O56315 2004
811'.6--DC22
2004010944

Alice James Book gratefully acknowledges support from the University of
Maine at Farmington and the National Endowment for the Arts. ❦

Cover image: Vincent van Gogh [1853-1890] D11V/1962. *Avenue With Poplars*
F 1239. Nuen, 1884. Courtesy of Van Gogh Museum (Vincent van Gogh
Foundation), Amsterdam.

Contents

(

ACKNOWLEDGEMENTS

☾

Grateful acknowledgement is made to the editors of the following journals and anthologies, in which some of these poems first appeared:

Center: A Journal of the Literary Arts: "Snow Angels," "Near the Heart of Happening"
Crazyhorse: "For Llamas," "Theories of Implication"
CutBank: "Something Like Blood"
The Mid-America Poetry Review: "Tonasket Elegy"
NEO Revista: "And Upon the Earth No Wind," "Listening Out"
Northern Music: Poems about and inspired by Glenn Gould, edited by J.D. Smith (John Gordon Burke, 2001): "Glenn Gould on My Mountain"
Ploughshares: "St.Francis at the Fire," "His Voice Had Grown Softer Each Day"

I would like to thank all those who have lent their generous guidance and assistance, including Dara Wier, Jack Gilbert, Greg Pape, Patricia Goedicke, Henriette Goodman, Rita Rich, Joseph Fletcher, Mark Wootton, and Nat Herold.

You know, people who do not believe
in the sun, in surroundings like this,
are godless.

—Vincent Van Gogh

do not fear the snow fear not the lion
or the moon anymore not the moon
shadows in the trees things without names
carry me from the freezing night
carry me from the fire the lungs the wheezing
the clabbered air scent of alder in wet snow of blue
spruce split to the core and a gust across
the mouth of a well deep down frozen
that gives back no light devil what have you
in your hands what place you on my tongue
it is you have made me wander empty
countless fields snowplows grinding down
the dark berms to believe not the
moon I fear man was made by the word
and man knows death by the word who do you
say I am shadowless the maple falls away
the wretched oak shudders what have you placed
on my tongue skins filled with fire our bodies
laid down which is the scent of god rising
and after the fire only teeth are left

☾

Gunshot in river-mist.
A mime of geldings

round the paddock
and the world draws in, serried

by weather,
sheaved and sundered.

A tractor echoes off a basanite bluff—
I for my part will go down singing,

have come thus far,
windbreak disavowed of leaves.

I'm polite, say yes and yes again
for I have so loved this world—

ash through which a mare meanders
blackens in the light,

feed bins upturned, glistered—
we want so much

to alter nothing,
the cloven paths that seep into water—

each heart
hydrant for the Lord.

I want to build my house
in you, phantom in the song-light.

Starlings unsilence,
jay-crows gloss a bone-stack

and I will not close my eyes
to the flame held before me,

O fire—of human
And not.

FOR LLAMAS

If you want to understand the beauty of llamas
you have to struggle with the dead.
You have to slip your arms beneath their ribs,
lock your hands together
and stagger with them
across a concrete floor out into cold wind,
through thistles, brown and brittle cheet grass,
your head against their collarbone
your face so close to their face
that you breathe for the both of you,
your breath glistening the fine hairs along a cheek
as you use your weight against their weight
and skin your knuckles
and the bridge of their nose
on a pile of rough-cut hemlock boards
and catch their elbow on a nail on a post
and curse when your arms get shaky
and your lungs burn
you drop them
apologize
and leave them lying on the gravel
let freezing rain glaze their awkward lips
and back the rusty blue Ford pickup up
and let it idle
crank the defrost
scrape the ice from the windshield
and drop the tailgate
and pick them up again
and lay them down again
in crusted snow and bailing twine in back,
their head resting on the spare
and throw a blue tarp on,
strap it down with shroud line
and throw a few heavy boards on for weight
and rest a while, listening to the AM

it is then that the llamas
come towards you
from the back of the field
through the snowdrift that remains,
past the lean-to and the barn,
past the feeders
and the new brown salt blocks in the salt houses,
past the round pen for breaking horses
and they will move without shadows
and you will know the ice in their matted hair
and you will smell them
as they smell you
as they lean their necks across the fence
and they will breathe out
and you will see it
and they will look at you
with their eyes filled with pastures of another world
and you not knowing what it is you are waiting for.

Pigeons erupting from a barn.
Twenty-three ewes
stand at once, ice chunks
clinking in their wool.
I call, soft, call loud
but the mare treads the snow blue
and I am born to constant
hazard. Wood becomes
more than wood simply
by its burning. Steam
rises up from the land—
I call but do not move.
The moon rising shines even
upon all things and I can't tell
which is mare
and what's weather.
Silence in eaves ever after.

AUGUST

The Lord is a place
to dig down into.
To harvest and burn,
let go fallow—
row of potato plants
blooming, thick
shocks of sweet corn
in rain, zucchini,
alfalfa,
carrots and fresh dung,
tobacco
steaming in a night.
In the five years
since you went away
I have not looked
for the Lord.
Tonight where I walk
He comes to me.
Fifty acres of wheat
past golden,
cardinals on a wood gate
silent, hands
waiting to open
like thistles in a pasture
more silver than air,
or coyotes in a windbreak,
a pen of sheared sheep.

THEORIES OF IMPLICATION

It begins in the leaves,
a hush that precedes all weather.

A cool light that sharpens the scene.
The air, the barn

empty of birds.
The tractor not moved for days.

Aspen along the low field, by the creek,
say nothing all night

and they say nothing now
which is the truth I'm after.

The culvert has its own theory.
So does the salt house

and the half-tub of molasses
caked with mud.

With the grass trying to maintain
the hue of September

everything is almost as it should be.
A new scent has entered the pasture—

an urgency that tempts like oats beneath a trough
for now I am come home

but all gates are left undone—
all windows empty.

I need you to get me a ticket, he said.
For what, I asked, waking at the foot of his bed.
For the train, he said. They say I need a ticket.
Except for the small lamp the room was dark.
The air was cool and clear. The first night of September.
Do you know who they are, I asked
and he said, oh yes. They are smiling and waving—
I haven't seen them for so long.
They want me to climb on board. . . . I need my ticket.
I want to give you a ticket, I said.

The foal hangs halfway out
and the mare strains
but can't push anymore.
I bring a bucket of cold river water
across the field. Haboo
I say in her ear,
what the Skagit children said
when the storyteller stopped:
keep the story going.
They said it with clamor,
with hands and voices
louder each time
but I am soft with it,
cool water on her neck.
Haboo I say reaching in
where the hips have locked
as she groans and falters.
Haboo for the shanks I grab
and jerk, for the spine
popping and the hips coming free.
Haboo for the foal lying in the dirt
as the mare nudges
and cleans its body
as the breathing stops.
Haboo as the body cools
as we stay with it after
as light begins,
as I regard the still air,
the meadowlark, the weight
of its bright singing.

A Tone Struck. Still Ringing

For I am equal to the weight of all things,
so sayeth the Lord.

Steam rises up from backs of llamas,
the barn, the weathered wood.

Maple blood their leaves.
In the struggle, what is seen

is carried over and held.
Fence posts blacked by fire,

the moon, small, late-rising,
A bridle hung inside out, froth-stained,

cob-webs on barbed wire,
a glistered heap of dung.

Lifted, onward—
hand-pump sheathed in rain,

hay rake broke down, rusted—
a bell far off—

that the words are not lost,
that apples crushed, rotting on a right-of-way

remain as they are
working deeper into the heart, the heart

overflowing with hemlock planks, shavings
from hooves fresh-shod—

we sing, are riven.

The day begins
& it's too nice for words.
My mother touched my hand.
If I had a lover, she'd be here.
I think the fish are calling
but it's the wind not whispering through trees
but across the neck of a horse
tangled in wire.
Willows grab my line & send the message
I was never wanted here. I was told one time
my father could whip the life back into rocks.
I kiss the horse and cry.
The other bank is posted with bottles
I never left—but want to. The sun sets
like a welt across the ass
& if I had a lover
she'd leave me. I tell myself I will act
man enough for mother to kiss me
when I come home with nothing but my hands.

In Chesaw Falling Behind

Orchard: nets of starlings rise.
Rain shakes loose—

ghost-seeds
in a ghost month.

A man from the far end sings
a language I do not know—

pours diesel in old tires,
sets to pruning branches.

And I, I lie on my back,
hands in gravel. I close my eyes.

Smoke wafts apple wood, then cherry—
and what the song says

I say. Wet weeds
soak into me one sprig at a time.

A fence screeks, tightens
and a herd bawls by.

He steps on a ladder—I know it's wood
by the way it doesn't ring out.

Branches drop to the fire.
A few stray bricks pop in the crackle.

In fields behind
schick, schick, schick of sprinkler pipe—

I sit up—listen for echo.
What the wind does, slowly, I do.

Arc Welder's Son

O furnace, your face
has always been
lost to me, sunk
in the blue brilliance
of your forged world.
Your hands
slag-pocked leather
scabbards,
your voice a wire-feed
ticking off the yards—
you have
a hermit's back,
a tinsel I-beam shadow.
Tell me, does
the militia in your brain
conspire
against you?
Do you flare each night
along the ramparts
through smoke of a
million flux-rod
torches?
There is one rule
to alchemy:
pure elements do not
tarnish. Consider
the democracies of
flume, scrap, and braze.
The cooling republic
of pewter,
expanding like America.
Consider fire,
that all things must
rise through it.
Listen to the fire,

to the plebes, to the fire.
Hard metal breeds
hard metal. What
oration will stave off
the closing rebels?
Plate your bastions
with purest silver.
Set coffers
before the bellows,
oil vats on the hob.
The skrick of a striker,
the pop-hiss
of oxy-acetylene
being trued
will give vague auguries
of victory
but to whom?
But my heart
is not like
your heart.
The darkness
that comes after fire.

Windless dark, not night,
cleanness after the moon.
Honest dark. Darkness on its own
leading into other things.
A mare wheezes in a far stall
of a far barn and
I think of that as a place
not yet filled with longing—
a home. Like llamas walking in snow
and what's beneath showing through.
The moment after coyotes
and how a heart pounds in that place.
Between trains bellowing along
a shallow river. Between sorrows.

SNOW ANGELS

The barn is a story we've taken refuge in,
the one where the ghosts never arrive.

We wait anyway
since the weather demands it.

Strike a match and nothing disappears,
nothing leaps out, either.

Snow is a verb with certain ideas in mind,
it settles on the fringe of your coat.

Give me your hands.
The wind has a way of saying things

no longer self-evident.
Since the barn does not repeat itself

I will. Your hands,
they are remote and necessary.

With the temperature this close to zero
everything is at risk.

This is not a story
we can leave untouched.

Daylight is five mares straining
the wires as I pass. A depth
of starlings tilted toward earth.
You call me a liar
and I walk through a razed field
after rain, a week of no rain,
trying to get it right, clear and ringing.
Horseflies rise from the past.
I am not gentle do not
sing. A lamb skull
slaked with moss gives way
beneath my foot. Yellowjackets
glisten violent in their arcs
and I let them. Poplar
unhand themselves of leaves.
Bone, we say. Ghost.
But I think of their hearts thickening.
A brightness in the wood.
A bearing and cadence
against all weather.
As a barn falls slowly in.
As tin curls and is driven back
down under the earth. Wind
blows black dust about me
but what does that prove? I whisper
and pick a handful of unburned weeds.
When I return to the paddock
there is blood on the wires.
But no horses.

The Lambs, the Fire

It is not for the lambs to ascend
from a dead form into the rain.
For fire does not consume,
it alters. Smoke is simply
smoke. The delicate
stillborn heads settle in the flame.
The damp wool sears.
When we dance
nothing comes of it
but the dance. Not to rise up
but smolder down
into ember, into ash.
When the fire slackens
we throw on diesel.
We pull more lambs from the tailgate,
their legs slick with birth.
Like cordwood, Mike says
as we pour on more diesel,
as the flames dim then flare.
We wait, throw on more lambs, more diesel.

What Comes to the Body and Lifts It
Is Sometimes Not the Spirit

Three days in the earth
and the spirit holds off,
and the moon does not rise.
El Greco painted angels
attending and angels
stacked overhead, the body
not knowing what comes next—
a white bird nearer, then away.
In Chagall there is the body
and whiteness only—
houses overturned,
a ladder leaned against light—
still the spirit witholds.
We're left alone to find
approximations for the truth.
Anna wasn't ready for how
the pain would be
after they removed
tumors from her breast.
She sat in a tub of cooling water
unable to wash herself.
So much tearing, she said,
my body flailing on the table.
I cradled her head in one arm
and laid her back.
Not until Thomas put his hand
in the wound did fire descend.
I rinsed shampoo from her dark hair,
tilted her head
to wash her neck.
Anna standing in the cool air.
Her smile as I kneel,
dry her feet.

Sludge heart. Pot-metal heart. Scree...
Some leaves fell. Schlock heart. Chill-
blain heart. Piss-stain heart. Gelded
heart. O heart incontinent. 24 carat
electroplate heart. *Cicadas were silent.*
Bumper-sticker heart. Foul-mouth
stink-bomb heart. Black. Black. Black.
And I sang all day. Drop-dugged wolf-
bitch heart. *And held birds in my*
hands. Thistle heart. Briar heart. Poison-
ivy heart. *And fish took council.*
Exiled heart. *My heart.* Trick-weighted
plumb-bob heart. *O heart.* O heart. FLAME.

In the Kingdom of Birds

Starlings will rise before me,
blue jays will shade my eyes,
sparrows will sweep the path
for my feet are willing, but tender.
And I will walk all day.
I will seek out the ovenbird
that I may eat of its sweet bounty,
and the nuthatch will weave me garments of grass
for my clothes are borrowed and threadbare,
and flax belongs to no one.
And I will liken myself to a fox sparrow,
an uncommon migrant of hedge and ditch.
I will consort with bohemian waxwings.
And I will sing for yellow-breasted chats
for they are good birds and worthy of a better song.
I will salute the American robin,
because I am a cowbird raised among meadowlarks.
In the hot rain, in cold rain,
in the snow, I will walk,
and I shall be as knight errant in the kingdom of birds.
The goldfinch will not abandon me
and the grackle will not chide the red tanagers of my heart
which give a burry chip-churr.
And I will say grateful things to crows.
O, my soul is a hermit thrush.
And the killdeer won't shy away.
Snipe will not plead for me.
Mourning doves will sit silent on the powerlines,
and the blackbird—
the common,
red-winged, yellow-headed,
the bobolink—
and the magpie
will not conspire against me.
Ravens will not dishearten me,

and I will pray with the vesper swallow,
and the falcon will grant me passage,
and I will be of service to pipits and titmice,
and I will not abandon my heart to the kingfisher
though he dives deep and keeps both eyes open,
and I will weep before blue herons,
and the blackburnians, the redstarts
and crossbills will nest in my eyes.
And this is how I will come to you.

GEARING HOUSED IN TWILIGHT

You know it's a question of fortune
that I concern myself with birds.
Not as structures of ornament
or discord
as the trumpets in Mahler,
but as the actual augury.
The soft whirring in the nests
that bring forth morning,
cardinals, doves,
kestrels and kites,
and the cruelty
that I am equal to.
The ham-hammering
of those variegated wings
into the thing
behind the thing.
As I am with geldings,
with moonlight.
As the miner's life depends
upon the constant
singing of the canary
to bring him down and up again.
Like Audubon.
Or Cameron, dying, his mind
filling with the trumpets
of his rare swan. Because
nothing lasts.
Not even lasting.

COME YOU WHITE MARE, COME STRIDING

In the hour before birds
In the naming of a few stars
In a few leaves fallen
In ash, ember, Come—
In the *splick, splick* of a water trough
For in this late month—
I hear so clearly for the first time
Crickets, the weeds—
In mist seeping in from the river
In field, in bone
You white mare
In rain that peens a curved world flat—
Shadow among shadows
Among voices, Come—
Through every weather between us
Come O come you white mare
Come thunder, come silent
Come peal, come sweep, come striding

GLENN GOULD ON MY MOUNTAIN

There are no pianos in heaven.
Cold rain rains down.
So many days rain on the scree
of my mountain.
I sit with the fugues
so the white hands might gain in me.
Like lions in moonlight
back and forth across the clearing.
Like Alaric through Rome.
Not the burning and plunder
but the morning three days after.
I turn up the finale at the edge of winter.
Gould hums where the piano fails.

BARN-CLEANING

A pigeon topples down,
cocks a dazed head.
I catch it, try snapping its neck
like a wet towel in air.
Stupid bird! Goddamned bird!
An alien eye.
I set the bird's head
against a flat rock.
Wings beat my ankle
but I do not rise.
Four and twenty birds
twitch in a barrel.

Tonasket Elegy

I.

The screen door a telegraph for the wind.
Ghost-layer of green on the fields.
Slowly now, the body begins
to believe in itself.
I walk all morning up and down the stairs
without tiring. I whisper
and that is enough,
I think, for now. It is April.
The orchards unfold as if God
might fall asleep at any moment. Forever.
In the morning there is still frost at work
on the blossoms.

II.

Death bides its time, durable flower.
I leave this candle dark.
As if the world started over,
as if different pleasures mattered this time around
the wind clears the aspen of delicate things.
It will rain soon. On the north hill it is winter
less and less. I no longer pretend
to be important. A pane
rattles in the window.
A shard of plaster breaks on the floor.
I breathe out unafraid.

III.

This is the house, hillside overwhelmed by April.
Here the sound of mice between plank-wood and tin—
the foundation settling to the center of the world.
There are things you can never trace back.
There is not one beginning. I run my fingers along my ribs
where cartilage and bone are mending.
One bird sings, then silence.
Evening begins in every direction.
I run my hands through the dust wanting a few stars
to come into view from there, where you are.

MONTANA MOUNTAIN POEM

At this hour
there is
nothing that can save you

Not another's
past, nor thin air
we climb into—

A back room
in the attic
of a grave

Sound
of wind on scree

Brother,
there is no
sound like that sound
in all the rest of this world

And above us
no stars—

There are of course
thousands
even millions of stars

But not now.

I close the simple flowers
and bid the moon now rise
for Death is not my harbor.
And I walk among derelict combines
that they might know
and come unafraid.
In mulberry small birds sleep.
Hornets enter one by one the districts
of their hidden city.
A fence dissolves. Reappears.
Oaks lean into the darkness,
into the light
bedded in a ditch.
That the chorus preserve us
as frost presses down
with equal weight and tenor.
That shadows breathe of their own
existence. That this heart
not fail. And these hands.
And those hands. That the moon move
and the earth move
as it was in the beginning.
I remember the alfalfa
and stacks of hewn wood—
as I remember that world
pouring into this.

How calmly the snow devoured the new houses,
the yardlights, your lips, your hair.
It was like watching a fire
from inside out. Even the spruce
were unaware and happy
until I mentioned the conspiracy.
And later when I could not find you
I did not call your name.
I unfolded all your clothes
and laid them in the yard.
The snow smiled, sharpened its teeth.

Frost on the white barn
but not on the red.
Frost on alder more white
than on thistle and dung.
Against snow in the pasture
where I walk clicking
my tongue among many sparrows rising.
Between brightness and weight.
How in trees wind turns air silver.
Ice on the water trough,
ewes breathing against it.
Green oak smoldering on a burn pile—
smoke more white than frost—
the whiteness of farewell—
the difference between snow untrampled
and sparrows over churned-up snow—
shadows deep and rough-hewn.
A mare coming slowly forward—
leaning into me when I scratch her neck.
The smell on my hands after.

In the Far and in the Near

I.

Strains of starlings rise
from neck-high sea-green wheat—

a few words the land
gives up, a few weeds bent

in any wind whatever—
a tractor idles down

a stone-boat smolders, laden,
a Torino hood pulled by chain—

as land is cleared, reworked—
an ice age picked by hand

and dumped in Kerwin's ravine—
the subtle declensions of light

against the far trees,
our shadows stretched with the day-work—

shovel, pickaxe, twenty-pound tamping bar,
the clutch easing out on the tractor,

exhaust flume blackening—
denominators of salt, smudge, and shoulder.

II.

Sleight-of-wind cast upon corn
and every maple, the settle

and shift of geldings in the pens,
crazed flight paths of swallows

meaning storm. Far
and near the delicate orations

of the lark. Far
and near again and now

the rain.

III.

Five nights I've listened for the owl's returns—
the many that mean hunger

and the one meaning feast—
blue smell of winter in the oak—

five mornings I've glimpsed my face
in the eyes of hobbled geldings—

a radio evangelist shouts *what is left
is left is left*—

I close my eyes.
That is Orion, I mutter,

but where shall I put
Cassiopeia?

How It Is to Go On
as One of the Not Chosen

As kreep-slats for the lambs
that are chosen,
as the steel race built
for breeding, keep me
like that. Of constant use
and function, alive
for the simple things
that they might have witness,
like pigeons brothering the air,
crickets in the noon wheat
and the darkness,
the apples we eat, the lips
we crush, the salt laced upon the body
against the black dirt
of a ditch bank, the steady
ruin of the bright magnolia.
Make me something more
than what I am as I wait for you
past bright, past beautiful,
the leaves beginning to turn,
and horrible night here in this place—
the residence I have of me,
the fine house
I could've been.

Canticle for the Landscape of One Hill and One Tree

by virtue of the land around
by virtue of the day
coldness putting edge to simple things
elm-leaf berm magnolia wire
how light makes the world apt
for ravage for the heart I have
as if I have no heart steel bells
ringing twenty-nine times
for everything my body a fistful
of dust tell me when will you come
listen there are things
I must not tell you such things
close by and by your own hand
sounds of pigs being troughed
sound of slaughter

VERNAL

Snowing now
that tacky
New England snow,
redressing
even the scrawniest oak.
There's a red bird
flicking the rhododendron
and I wonder if
that bird knows
it's beautiful—
nothing more than
resting
on a branch.
Still you sleep,
the scars on your breast
less purple now—
ah, but you, there—
the time
we kissed
on Fifth Avenue,
saying yes
this is how our
story begins—
you bent your neck
forward,
hair smelling
of ash—
that sigh as you
turn in your sleep away
from where I watch you—
this much but only so—
hand that has touched me
ten thousand times—
blue-veined
and thriving against

this darkness
and I
who have come
so broken—
your shoulder
in what moonlight
remains after
morning, the dark
matted strands
of hair, your breathing
hurried—
what dream
has put you here?
A sparrow sings
because no one cares—
for you are not
cardinal, not
breath-taking flash
but steadfast
with fine-boned love—
and see, the bird
has vanished—
the snow turns rain in the light
but still
after all this everything—
each gust accountable
in the land
that's in my heart
and how far I have wandered,
and I will not touch you
and I will go knowing
beneath clabbered snow
a green world readied—
for the delicate and the lordly
rise from the same house.

LOSING SOMETHING IMPORTANT

You hear ice tightening in trees—
great birds driving through the wilderness.
And when the beasts shift in their stables
it is with a steadiness that once belonged
to paradise. Plant me in your soil she said
and I will become your earth.

Gentleness We Lay upon the Earth That Rises Up as Starlings

Steam in the air where the earth is melting.
Cover crop and corn stubs reaching
for the light. As light
on this body also, scent of new
lamb on my hands (what if there were
no gate? I bring so little.
A few thistles and not much feast).
Mist and the coming dark make the air
taste more and more of magnolia. As the tree
is always magnolia, blooming or naked,
flourishing, stump, or memory.
As the woman smiling,
braced against the trunk
for the force of him coming from behind
(did I search too hard? Was I not
a body?), and the rain in the night,
the late-coursing distillate moon
indifferently nursing any field.
The widow next door
plants a garden with oxygen
on her back. Pushes down seeds,
rests on a cane, says
"I plant early on faith." As if I could stay here
and know more than just
sleep and fodder,
sowing and threshing.
Or will I be a rosebush
gone feral by the front steps?
So many blossoms that smell more
of air than petal or desire.
Oh Lord, who art above each rain.
Lover of cripples, the deaf, the blind,

protect me not. I who wanted to be
spark-on-the-flesh. Who sang
lamb oh lamb, the threshold.
Put no lemon in my hair to make me shine.

SAUDADE

And what is given in return?
There was a darkness then
shaped by swallows—
a brightness given completely
by a few thistles and the moon.
But who's to say if the heart lives up
to what's placed in it?
Soon the trees will alter—
the earth grows small and bare.
Surely everything tender
is not granted. There is silence
among crickets meaning storm—
I spread flame in the windrow
to vetch the underbrush
but not damage the spruce
as I glimpse your face from
across the fire. The roaring heard,
the burning.

CANTICLE FOR THE DAY-LABOR

temper me make me plow blade
an implement for the deep earth
a pleasure in the sowing
and if I bleed make it plentiful
make it sweet like honey
like a train spike through the skull
and I will push the land
and dispatch winter
for the veins of my lord
are always open

PROSPETTIVA DI SPEDITIONE

The roan, the weeds,
white birds, and Anna.
Steel bells tolling, tolling
making a mess of me—
rye half-masted in the fields.
Living, says Henriette,
is one transparency
laid upon another.
Maybe, I think, but isn't it strange
how wind blows where corn
once was, still trying
to make that sound?
Ghost-corn, maybe.
And if I'm the vanishing point?
Or made of embers
the wind cannot touch.
This is a sky that harbors
and does not damage.
Puts birds there
again and again. Small
and singing. Hawk and resting.
The maple are violet in this distance.
Tobacco barns
hold slats open for the dark,
and fox are digging dens
in the dry ditch bank,
the nascent calling of sheep,
and the slat-ribbed oxen
nudging for feed, the roan,
and already what I yearned for most
has lost all definition.

Untitled

You are but a shape, moulded clay.
I? A cleaver through a singing bird.

The Vessels of Each of Us Knocking Against the Night

In the window, in the vines outside, in the stench
of llamas, the silage, the lambs new-born, wire
rusted and fence post broken, the ditch, the steam,
the elm, the crows, the field tilled
and the field held fallow, the roadway, apples
fallen, crushed, set writhing with worms, dung bejewelled
by shit-flies, trimmings from manes drifting the gust,
in the light before evening, after rain,
the intermittent and solid season, the seven ducks
flicking water, coyote den in the far bank,
in cracked hooves of the weather-worn roan, whatever
sings and then is silent, what sings on, furrow
and dead furrow, tractor by the river, red barn
fifty-two cows long, roiling the seed, splaying
the sod, in stars above the river, planes
above the river, cars between fields droving cattle
back and forth, one dog yapping and one dog cooning,
in the interchange and flux, and in these things
if you look you will see me, and if you do not see me,
you will see what I have seen. Our eyes will lock.
For a moment we will not shatter in the light.

Rain on deadfall and on living wood.
No sun yet, no sun tomorrow, a light
with every shadow siphoned out—
and yonder windbreak breaking. Winter
and I naked on the bed trying
to remember the birds, the gradual
discord of the fields that has left me
this slight authorship of dirt.
I remember everywhere each thing humming
and doves rising up. The humid river.
Peepers omniscient in the ripening trees. Their song
all day warning of night, the stunning
heartbreak of the ordinary. Don't close your eyes
to this, I whisper in the heave
of hips, the light, fingers
in my mouth. I remember
the pliant air slaked with pollen,
the oscillate moon through cloud—
seven white ducks calling for the one
not returning. You rising after
smiling at the wetness on your belly.
Scent of copper. Scent of loam.

LITTLE BROOK FARM,
SUNDERLAND, MASSACHUSETTS

See the winter. Pale and brown.
Dirt road where ice should be.
Stringlets of dust rise from every field
and enter the wind that comes full
off the river, shearing the last
leaves from yellow birch and bog oak
and heaves the rough-hewn walls
where he tends the matted and rank
and steamy beasts in the unlit space
of a barn. Shadows fling from the rafters,
clatter down and peal
into that great and oscine wind.
Haboo he says to calm a mare's flinch,
to llamas testing at the hay.
And so the days go on like this,
hands upon the baling twine,
upon the hooves gauging wear.
And the wind does not stop. And death
does not stop riding hard for this body.
When I close the doors, there is a brightness
fitted to the stars and stars only.

If I'm Not a Garden

I'm in the pasture calming down the mares,
calculating what might be taken
by the hurricane as sacrifice.
Anything not rooted might be taken.
If I'm taken? There is a power in me
I do not understand. Terrifying
is the clarity by which I see,
as though each thing ignited by candles
inside. If I'm not a garden,
but a shadow pleading for stone,
rock, tree, or standing wall to cast against
in order not to vanish,
what then? The air is crisp. Sheep click their teeth
on blades of grass. Does vanish mean
to arrive elsewhere? A place perhaps
to flourish, to withstand? Maybe Freiburg
among the almost perfect German forests.
Maybe Ohio.

At the Hour God Speaks
in the Key of Longing

And the words were our leaves
and winter was a quieting
and the wind moved us
to gain bearings with the truth
the shadows are the night's way
to cling to what the light discards
or the earth compacted by thaw
so the weeds have something to grow against
at the hour God speaks in the key
of longing, low sounds like pigeons
dying in the muck of a barn
as trees yield their resin to the light
and I wear a dark shirt
on a hot day remembering not
the bounty but the intervals
by which harvest was had
and how from mud at your feet
I fashioned every starling
and happiness was every field, every barn,
two silos leaning toward the trees
your handprint on the window
some rural savant banging the fenceline
and I followed where you needed to go,
I the shard, the furnace, the dust on the road
that blurs your vision
and before I am done I will slit the throats
of your maple trees, I will solder
every bird to the sky, I will staple
the sun's mouth to the tempest
because I can, because it is in me, because
I have written it, and I will pull
the lamb from the ewe of my father's flock
and I will mark your ear with blood
and your heel, and your face with ash

and I will not spare the peacock or the hen
and you will be a gelding stalled by the plow
and you will call me tornado and blossom-weevil
and fire will be the inn-keep
and ice will be the magistrate
and the tufted titmouse will gasp beneath the sun
for there will be no shade and no bark to cling to
and the interstates will buckle in my hand
and I will raise your cities from mud
and raze them with rain
and there will be no country,
citizens of nothingness,
the brightness of the lamb,
the darkness of the lamb,
the sky with its need and its plenty.

Brown corpses of thistle in a greening field.
The beauty and the birds that court every carnage
unraveling the dead, calming the dying
as the wind gathers its spoils of dust,
and tulips, their painful blooming
unlatch the dank accretions of last year's leaves,
the green nubs that will become August,
king of the months, and every insect emerging
hard-wired for the sun, little lamb, little llama,
branches stacked and granted to the fire,
smoke from the hollows and floodplain of the river,
one barn with a new tin roof, one barn freshly fallen,
curls of trimmed hoof on the uneven floor of a stable,
hemp rope through the sockets of a skull, a fox den filling
with water, white feathers on the water, the small
distances of the fields, stone walls, trees,
a tractor chuffing under the labor of the plow,
the lamb, the llama, nursing in the aftermath.

☾

Recent Titles from Alice James Books

The Devotion Field, Claudia Keelan
Into Perfect Spheres Such Holes Are Pierced, Catherine Barnett
Goest, Cole Swensen
Night of a Thousand Blossoms, Frank X. Gaspar
Mister Goodbye Easter Island, Jon Woodward
The Devil's Garden, Adrian Matejka
The Wind, Master Cherry, the Wind, Larissa Szporluk
North True South Bright, Dan Beachy-Quick
My Mojave, Donald Revell
Granted, Mary Szybist
Sails the Wind Left Behind, Alessandra Lynch
Sea Gate, Jocelyn Emerson
An Ordinary Day, Xue Di
The Captain Lands in Paradise, Sarah Manguso
Ladder Music, Ellen Doré Watson
Self and Simulacra, Liz Waldner
Live Feed, Tom Thompson
The Chime, Cort Day
Utopic, Claudia Keelan
Pity the Bathtub Its Forced Embrace of the Human Form, Matthea Harvey
Isthmus, Alice Jones
The Arrival of the Future, B.H. Fairchild
The Kingdom of the Subjunctive, Suzanne Wise
Camera Lyrica, Amy Newman
How I Got Lost So Close to Home, Amy Dryansky
Zero Gravity, Eric Gamalinda
Fire & Flower, Laura Kasischke
The Groundnote, Janet Kaplan
An Ark of Sorts, Celia Gilbert
The Way Out, Lisa Sewell
The Art of the Lathe, B.H. Fairchild
Generation, Sharon Kraus
Journey Fruit, Kinereth Gensler
We Live in Bodies, Ellen Doré Watson
Middle Kingdom, Adrienne Su
Heavy Grace, Robert Cording

Alice James Books has been publishing exclusively poetry since 1973. One of the few presses in the country that is run collectively, the cooperative selects manuscripts for publication through both regional and national annual competitions. New regional authors become active members of the cooperative, participating in the editorial decisions of the press. The press, which historically has placed an emphasis on publishing women poets, was named for Alice James, sister of William and Henry, whose fine journal and gift for writing went unrecognized within her lifetime.

Typeset and Designed by Dede Cummings
Printed by Thomson-Shore